For my parents
Sixt and Gisela

1

Acknowledgments

Every book is a team effort but often the author may find oneself alone, this cannot be said of this project. Words alone cannot express my indebtedness to the hard work of the many people who helped to bring this book to life, the least I can do is give credit where credit is due.

Jack Cwele - an unfailing coordinator and ever patient interpreter.

Warren Green got me out of a jam with his explanatory drawings.

Anna Shaw and Caron Pearce sacrificed a lot of their valuable time hunting down the grammar devils in the manuscript.

Inkosi Ngema, Inkosi Byiela, Inkosi Malinga, Inkosi Fakude, Inkosi Gasa, Mr. Graham Stewart and all their people, shared a wealth of information with me over the years, about the dying Zulu culture, took me to places and happenings, that otherwise would have stayed in the dark for me.

Professor Louis de Clercq from the Department of Anthropology and Development Studies of the University of Zululand, was consulted on the contents.

My deepest thanks go to my dear parents in Germany, who set me on the way and persistently removed hurdles of all kinds in my path, enabling me to publish this booklet.

This handbook was not written by me alone. My very best friend, my wife Kathleen, uncomplainingly endured endless hours on her own at all times of the day and night, leading me back on track with loving criticism and pushing me on when I wanted to give up. She went over the rough translation, wrote and rewrote parts of it and put it into the form that you now hold in your hands. Her name should be quoted as the author - not mine.

Uli von Kapff
Durban
June 1997

"...Our party were received by King Shaka in a friendly manner, but with that air of haughty indifference which might be expected from the Napoleon of Eastern Africa, before whom everyone was prostrated.

A hundred thousand warriors, whose victories had annihilated nations, who had fought in fields saturated with the blood of their slain comrades, knelt at his feet, and to them his words were as the mandate of their deity.

Our present excited neither pleasure nor curiosity. He received it with listless indifference, causing it to be thrown aside, and commenced a desultory conversation, asking questions of King George's dominions, if he had as many cattle and as many warriors as he had, expressing his wish to be on friendly terms with King George, and would give his white people every attention; repeating that if any of them gave them any offence or insult, he would kill them all, men, woman and child..."

The Natal Papers of 'John Ross' from Charles R. MacLean

Amazi (Delicacy)

Curdled milk is one of the most desired staple foods of the Zulus and normally is not shared with anybody who does not belong to the family. This is strange as they share all other food. The milk is poured into gourds, leather pouches or baskets and left to stand until the contents has turned sour, which happens quickly in the climatic conditions of Zululand. Possibly this process is accelerated by the condition of the container as they may not be cleaned under any circumstances. Cleaning them would be considered extremely peculiar as every morning and evening fresh milk is added. The watery liquid is released through a small opening at the bottom of the gourd and the container is then topped up with fresh milk. This process is repeated until the bottle is completely filled with cottage cheese. The empty gourd is immediately used again for the next portion of amazi.

Food . 23

Ancestor Worship

Sacrificial bones - hut of the dead.

Zulus, like most tribes in Africa, pay tribute to the souls of the dead and make offerings.

Those left behind, still go to great lengths to bring the soul of the deceased home from the place of death, to the family kraal. When moving to a new home, old rituals are employed to settle the soul at the new abode.

The souls live in the spiritual world of *unkulunkulu* ("the greatest of the great" or God) but have second homes with their families. Ancestors are perceived as "guardian angels" and intermediaries between the living and unkulunkulu. To ensure this, the head of the family praises the deeds of the deceased and occasionally makes an offering.

If something negative should occur, such as an illness, a misfortune or death, then the *sangoma* (spiritual healer, medium) is consulted in order to ascertain whether this has been caused by witchcraft or, as a consequence of neglecting a spirit that wished to be remembered. There is either a

Protective wall of a Royal kraal.

subsequent witch hunt or an offering that is certainly not made in a submissive manner. One behaves in an incensed way and kills the sacrifice while chanting, for example:

"Why are you killing us, your children? Why do you turn your back on us? Here is your bull! Take it! Look after us as we also take care of you. Why did you bring illness to this child? You are greedy, you are looking for flaws. When you have killed us all, there will be nobody to look after you".

Armourer

Iron ore is not rare in South Africa and smelting and forging iron into spears and hoes was not a craft introduced by the white man.

Iron forgers usually led the lives of hermits, not only because of the noise and increased danger of fire but also because of the distrust they were met with. To give their weapons the magic power of an Excalibur the armourer used potent medicine, sometimes consisting of

Forging a blade.

Burning the blade into the shaft.

human organs and fatty tissue that they obtained from *umthakathi* (wizards). Whenever an adult or a child disappeared in mysterious circumstances, a black smith or his sinister accomplices were suspected.

The constant demand for weapons guaranteed the iron forgers their survival, otherwise one would have just got rid of them.

Baskets

Clay for pot making is not available everywhere, therefore, Zulu people weave baskets made of dried grass, thin rushes or lengths of telephone wire of different colours. These baskets are used as storage vessels for maize cobs, to transport kernels *(iquthu)* and as drinking vessels *(isichumo)* for the popular sorghum beer. The latter, decoratively woven beer mugs have a fixed place in most of the ethnological museums and private collections today. The material used for weaving is split strips of dried leaves from the Ilala palm tree, stained in almost all colours of the rainbow, by being placed in either a brew of roots, berries, cow-dung or other natural additives. Over long periods, skilful hands weave these thin strips into strong baskets with certain geometric designs. People initiated in this craft can read information regarding the producer or the owner by the depicted pattern.

Before the drinking vessel is used for the first time, the minute pores are closed from the inside with moist, coarse, maize flour, causing the palm leaves to swell and thereby sealing it.

Splitting palm leaves for weaving.

BASIC DESIGNS

 Triangle - Masculine

 Double Triangle forming hourglass shape Married man.

 Diamond - Feminine

 Double Diamond Married woman

 Zig-zag pattern (masculine) "The Assegais of Shaka"

 Series of Diamonds (Feminine) "The Shields of Shaka"

 Small squares or dots - a celebration of fruitfulness (i.e. good rains, good crops, many cattle, a new child.)

THE "MARRIAGE" DESIGN

A special basket is woven by the Bride, or a member of her family, as a gift from her to the Groom, which he will use at the Wedding as a beer-drinking vessel. The story of the marriage is woven for posperity, and for all to see - the more affluent the family, the more detailed the design woven into the basket.

Diamond - the Bride

The number of points round the outside of the design indicate the number of cattle paid for "labola" (Bride price)

Double triangle (Hour glass indicates that the groom has been previously married).

Battle of Blood River

The deceitful murder of the Voortrekker leader, Piet Retief and his one hundred strong delegation, by the Zulu king Dingane, started the most important military battle between the Boers and the Zulus - the Battle of Blood River on 16 December 1838. This blood-bath brought an end to the military power of the Zulus for a period of time, later led to the death of King Dingane and opened the land south of the Tugela river for unrestricted settlement by the Boers.

History 24

Battle formation

King Shaka was the most ingenious strategist on the African battlefields in the 19th century. Although initially outnumbered by far, he overcame with ruse and cunning much more powerful opponents and took possession of their land until there was no known adversary left. With his new close-combat spears, Shaka changed the naive skirmishes, which had been customary until then, into blood baths of incredible dimensions.

Apart from the deadly war spear he invented, he also perfected the battle formation, that had been unknown until then, the so-called "bull-horn" formation, which meant surrounding the enemy's army and butchering them mercilessly in close combat. His 50.000 warriors were organised according to age into regiments of 2.000 men each. The regiments of the younger and therefore more agile warriors flanked the battle troops of the

experienced veterans. At the time of enemy contact the young warriors ran to the sides, left and right, past the enemy and met at the rear end so that any escape route was cut off. The trapped opponents were pushed towards units experienced in war and massacred.

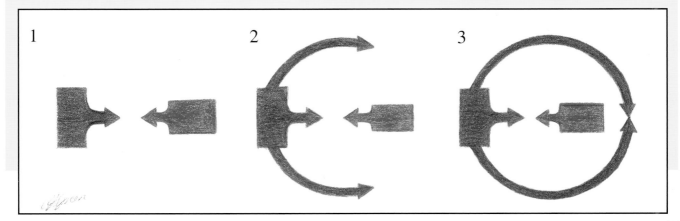

1   2   3

Battle of Isandlwana

In the first days of the Anglo-Zulu war of 1879, the British invading units suffered a catastrophic defeat which caused headlines throughout the world and has not been forgotten by the British to this day.

On 22 January 1879, the main military forces of the British were camped at the foot of Isandlwana hill in Zululand, not knowing that nearly 14.000 warriors were hiding in the vicinity. The commander of the powerful fighting units underestimated the fighting strength of the native people and therefore considered it unnecessary to take protective measures.

When the Zulus started their surprise attack against the invading troops, most of the ammunition of the British forces was still locked in boxes. The Redcoats fought courageously with their bayonets against a superior force armed with spears. A few hours later, approximately 1.000 warriors and 1.329 soldiers lay dead on the battlefield, and only a handful of British soldiers managed to save themselves by crossing the border river.

The Zulu monarch, King Cetshwayo, was involved in a defensive war and as a sign of his goodwill he did not attack the land of the whites that was then unprotected.

Kaleidoscope of artful beadwork.

Beadwork

Many tribes in Africa are known for their elaborate and impressive beadwork, and due to their love of beads the Zulu people take first place. The glass beads from Arabic and European traders were particularly coveted, as in the opinion of the native people, they were not only considered pretty but to be of a rather mystic origin. Many believed that they grew on magic trees, others insisted that they were taken from the sea. Their value far exceeded that of gold. For four beads a chicken was traded and for two to three kilos the fattest bull was bartered.

The smaller the beads the more one was prepared to trade in for them. The colour, too, determined the value. Red beads were of particular interest, followed by blue and then the less attractive white and black

Enjoying a pot of sorghum beer with friends.

Beer brewing

Traditional beer is made of sorghum and brewed daily by women.

The brewery can be picked out easily by the unusual structure of the hut: it is not completely thatched so that smoke can escape and the beer obtains enough oxygen for fermentation.

Sorghum beer *"Utshwala"* is very popular and equally enjoyed by old and young. The alcohol content lies between two and three percent, thus it is lower than that of western beer. It is an excellent thirst quencher, nutritious and even soothing for stomach ulcers.

Coarsely ground maize and sorghum is cooked to form a thick porridge, placed in shallow baskets and left standing in the open for one day to steep. On the second day, the softened grains are boiled in water to form a milky soup and dried sorghum is sprinkled over it. The large pot is covered with a sack or grass mat to keep out flies

Zulu crockery for sorghum beer.

and dust, then left to ferment for the day. On the third day, the brew is filtered through a large grass sieve and then served.

Sorghum beer has to be consumed on the same day otherwise it turns sour.

The alcohol-containing shells retained in the filtering process is fed to chickens and donkeys with amusing results.

Poorer families use the residue several times, however this makes the beer sour.

ones. Green and yellow beads were reserved for the chiefs, and usually only members of the royal household adorned themselves with these beads.

Before glass beads were introduced, the Zulu people used colourful little stones, sea shells, gold and copper baubles, ivory, bones, egg shells and colourful wood for their adornment.

9

Beer drinking

Before guests are invited to drink sorghum beer, the hostess will perform certain actions that are normally hardly noticed.

The ritual is always started by the woman who brewed the beer. She skims the froth off with a spoon-like sieve made of grass and pours it beside the foot ball size clay pot *(uKhamba) (picture 3)*. This is the offering for the spirits who always drink first. The contents are stirred with a small brush made of strong reeds to loosen the particles *(picture 4)*. Then a small hollowed gourd *(iNkheswa)* is filled and she demonstratively drinks in front of her husband and guests *(picture 5)* to prove that the beer can be consumed without any worry. *(In former times one simply invited the enemy for a reconciliation festivity and then poisoned them.)* It is then the host who drinks first to check the quality *(picture 6)*. Only once he is satisfied, are his guests served, in order of status, men first, then women and children last. All present, drink either directly from the clay pot or use a communal hollowed gourd which can easily hold half a litre or more. One holds the gourd with the right hand and places the grass lid under the chin with the left hand. It

5. *Testing for poison.*

6. *Quality testing by the host.*

4. *Stirring.*

3. *Offering to the spirits.*

2. *Start of the ritual.*

1. *Presenting the sorghum beer.*

is considered bad manners to drink while standing, and men take off their head covers.

Everybody takes a long drink, as it takes quite sometime for the communal calabash to make its round. As long as the emptied gourd is handed back with the opening pointing upwards it shall be filled again. A gourd returned with the opening upside down indicates *"the mouth is closed"*, having had enough.

The beer pot is covered with a grass cap *(Mbenge)* shaped like a soup plate, to prevent dust getting in. With this cap, host and guest communicate without uttering a word. If the guest places the cap on the pot pointing upwards he indicates to the hostess that the pot is empty and he would like to have it refilled. However, if the host places the cap in this way on the pot it signals the end of the beer ceremony, and nothing more is offered to drink. In this simple way the Zulu people end their festivities, and somebody who dares to help himself would be dealt with quite severely.

Burials

In rural areas traditional burials take place as in ancient times. The only person buried within the kraal is the patriarch, his resting place being in the cattle enclosure. Frequently the corpse is sown into the skin of a black bull and buried in a sitting position. Here the deceased is closest to his most valuable possession on earth, namely the cattle. Other relatives are buried outside the kraal. In former times the dead were simply hidden somewhere and left for the hyenas, vultures and ants.

Little importance is attributed to a corpse. It is the soul which is revered and constant offerings are made to secure lasting protection of the descendants.

If the chief died at a different place, then his soul is taken home. To achieve this, the family sends a delegation equipped with a small branch from a buffalo thorn acacia tree *(Ziziphus mucronata)*, to the place of death. There the spirit enters the branch and the delegation returns home. The person carrying the branch talks to the spirit throughout the journey and keeps him informed of all happenings. Beyond this, he is not allowed to participate in any other conversation, otherwise the soul might slip away. On the return journey a ticket is bought for the deceased, he is given a place at mealtime, in short, he is treated like a living person. On their arrival in the kraal his descendants place the branch in the cattle enclosure where it is eaten, his soul being absorbed in this manner. If the family moves residence, they take the spirits of the ancestors with them using a similar ritual.

Nguni cattle.

Cattle

The conventional Zulu man loves his cattle almost more than himself, and is prepared to risk his life for their protection. Cattle represent wealth, power, status and many more things than white people, with their different mentality could ever understand. A rural man without cattle is a poor soul. He can neither implore his fate-determining ancestors for a better fortune by means of sacrifices, nor may he marry a wife as he has not got the required *lobola*, the bride price of at least eleven beasts. Thus it is not surprising that most of the Zulu people hold their cattle very dearly. All ambition and energy is directed towards the upkeep and increase of the four-legged treasures. The most fulfilling moments for a Zulu man is the inspection of the herd returning home, or silently watching the animals as they graze in the carefully selected fields. The possession of cattle means food and clothing, indeed, all possible comfort and desirable luxury. The Zulu man spends his free time in the field enjoying his herd, and even chiefs or kings do not wish for a more enjoyable pastime. Irrespective of the size of the herd, the owner knows every individual beast equally as well as he knows his own children. He is so familiar with their spots, the shape of their horns and the characteristics of them, that the absence of one from a herd of a few hundred animals is immediately detected. This says a lot about the observation ability of the Zulu people, and the proverbial statement of a chief who does not know all his cattle, describes his incredible wealth.

Lobola ..
.... 37
Sacrifices
.... 43

Chief

The term chief, or the correct name being *inkosi*, is the general expression for the head of a family, a chieftain, a leader, etcetera. The inkosi is more than just a person giving orders, he is the father figure to his people, the source of their entire wealth, the symbol of the tribe and the one who determines the fate of his people.

An inkosi who had failed in the eyes of his king would have been condemned to death together with those under his authority.

Inkosi Ambrose Malinga.

Circumcision

Since the 18th century circumcision is no longer carried out among the Zulu people. The ruler in those days, King Dingiswayo, prohibited circumcision that was customary at that time, until all his wars would have been successfully concluded. As he was murdered at an early stage, this aim could not be reached, and the subsequent ruler, King Shaka Zulu, did not resume the custom for other reasons.

The Xhosa people living further south still practice circumcision rituals for boys in puberty, but the barbaric mutilation of the female genitals is unknown amongst the tribes in southern Africa.

Close Combat

iXhwa battle spear, Shaka's deadly weapon.

King Shaka demanded from his warriors a totally new type of warfare - close combat. In former times, the enemy faced one another at a distance of approximately fifty metres, letting loose the worst insults at each other, then threw spears at their opponents which were actually designed for hunting. The conflict usually ended when one side had thrown all their spears and started to retreat. This rather ridiculous kind of warfare was very ineffective and the losses on both sides were negligible.

Shaka instituted a new strategy by equipping his warriors with new close-combat spears *(iXhwa)* and by having them storm into the enemy lines. The attacker then hooked his large shield onto that of his opponent and pulled it to the side in order to expose part of the enemy's body, then drove in the blade of his spear. The opposition was not only shocked by this kind of unknown warfare but also at a total disadvantage with their backward throwing spears.

Provoking the enemy.

| Battle formation .... 7 |
| Weapons .... 56 |

Dancing

The Zulu people love dancing and singing, and a fair part of the day is spent on this healthy activity, from early childhood onwards. It is customary that only unmarried girls and young men dance, alternating in separate groups. While the girls dance, they are accompanied by the singing and clapping of the boys, then vice versa. Married women utter a shrill quavering as an expression of their joy, and some adult men occasionally break through the rows, wildly gyrating, beat their fighting sticks on their shields, as if they were attacking an invisible enemy. Typical of Zulu dances is the acrobatic performance of throwing one foot in the air to reach head height and then powerfully stamping the ground, which in the case of several dancers, makes the ground vibrate.

Bull dance by the men

This is a relatively new dance dating to the turn of the century, which originated between the narrow rows of beds in the mine barracks. At the end of their shift the mineworkers were more or less confined to their

Clapping to the beat.

War dance.

dormitories and experienced communication difficulties, as they came from all parts of southern Africa.

The joy in dancing and pride of the strong bull at home, was common to all of them. Thus they danced beside the bunk-beds and particularly liked to imitate a strong bull. Due to the lack of space and to prevent collision, all dancers had to execute the same movements and dance in formation. The arms held high, symbolises the extending horns of the bull, the feet are thrown to the height of the head and then powerfully stamped down on the ground. In this way, two quick steps are danced to the left and two to the right, all men closely together in a row, exactly as it used to be between the narrow rows of beds.

15

Bull dance by the girls.

Bull dance by the girls

When the young mineworkers spent their annual holiday with their families in the rural areas, they demonstrated the newly learnt dance to the people at home. The young girls liked the 'bull dance' and developed their own version of it.

Hunting dance by the men

Zulu men are passionate hunters and in former times were only armed with spears, clubs and axes when they went hunting. They did not only kill harmless antelope and wild boar, but had an eye on lions, buffaloes, leopards and elephants as well. This demanded a good deal of courage, which the hunters generated by dancing fiery dances for hours before setting off, imagining earlier successful hunting expeditions or imminent hunting scenes. While dancing they attack, retreat and imaginary animals are stabbed. Instead of spears the men use harmless sticks to prevent injuries during the aggressive gyrations.

Hunting dance by the girls

The women and maidens were, of course, happy about the safe return of their beloved ones and in gratitude they danced their version of the hunting dance.

Hunting dance by the girls.

Dance of the small shield

This is a rhythmical and very fast dance formation, dating back to Shaka's times when it was used to encourage military unity. Modern armies practise marching in uniformity, Zulu warriors do the same when dancing. Today it is the King's dance, usually performed at festive occasions.

umQhogoyo

This dance involves making faces, spasmodic shaking of the upper part of the body and particularly conspicuous shaking movements of shoulders, arms and chest.

African rattles made of cocoons.

Umbhekuzo dance

A dance resembling the ebb and flow of the tide. The men dance in rows, moving close to the spectators, stamp their feet and then retreat - as if going into close combat with the enemy and then immediately retreating. At both ends of the rows the dancers bend and lift up the back of their aprons, thereby exposing their buttocks.

Umbhekuzo dance.

Cheered into action.

umChwayo

Snakelike movements of the body accompanied by sonorous singing.

umGebhulo

The dancers seem to want to pull down the sky with their hands or climb up to it, on an imaginary ladder.

umGhubho

A very impressive war dance with spear and shield.

iliKhomba

This dance is done with graceful movements of the upper part of the body, with rhythmic swinging of a long decorated stick, accompanied by aggressive stamping of the feet.

iliKhomba dance.

umSombozo

Danced by the girls with continual bending and raising of the upper part of the body.

Dress

Men

Traditional dress for men consists of animal skins and feathers, the kind of skins indicate the social status of the person wearing them.

aMashoba:

The tufts of cows' tail are worn on the upper arms and below the knee joints, to make the person appear broadly built and thus more awe inspiring.

aMashoba

isiNene:

For the front apron, skins are cut into circular patches the size of large coins, and strung together through a centre hole by means of sinews. Some rows of these tassels cover the male genitals. The discs of skins are pressed tightly together to give the *isiNene* more weight and prevent it from opening in the case of abrupt movement, like dancing, as normally no clothing is worn beneath it.

iBeshu:

The apron covering the buttocks is made of calf-skin, which is soft and easily processed. Of course, the Zulus do not slaughter a calf for this purpose as it will grow into a valuable beast. They use the skins of stillborn or perished calves. The *iBeshu* comes in two different lengths:

Young men use knee-length versions for practical reasons as they would otherwise easily step on the tail-coat-like ends when dancing, running, fighting or working.

Older men who are spared these activities wear ankle length aprons as a sign of their dignity.

Headband:

Only married men used to wear them.

Ceremonial and everyday attire.

Leopard skin:

The leopard is considered to be king amongst the animals because it has the qualities attributed to those of a good leader. A leopard is independent, cunning, strong and invincible. If a leopard is killed, the skin has to be handed over to the king. Only the royal family, *indunas* (generals) and *chiefs* may wear leopard skins. The amount of leopard skin worn, however, is limited to the status of the respective person. Whereas the king can wear as much as he wants to, a relatively unimportant chief is possibly only entitled to don a small headband. In this way, one can immediately recognise the seniority of the wearer.

The average person may only adorn himself with a little leopard skin on his wedding day.

inJobo:

Long strings made of rare animals skins, worn on the hips, to demonstrate position and power.

Women

Single: An unmarried woman is proud of her body and is not ashamed of showing it. Irrespective of whether she is fat, thin or has a small or large bosom, she only wears a short skirt made of grass or beaded cotton strings. Beyond this she will spruce herself up with beadwork. The Zulus do not contribute any sexual meaning to the naked breast, it is rather the back of the upper thigh that excites men.

Engaged: If a young woman has chosen a man, she will let her traditionally short hair grow and cover her breasts with a decorative cloth. She does this out of respect for her future relatives and to indicate that she has been spoken for.

Married: The married woman covers her body completely, signalling to other men that she is taken. Another man's wife is regarded as absolute taboo and may not be touched by any other man. She wears the following clothes:

Topskirt:

Over the traditional skirt of cowhide a cloth in the dominant colours red, white and black is draped.

Festive dress of a maiden.

19

Hat:

Married woman wear a hat made of dried grass, often intertwined with red or white cotton thread. Size and shape of the hats differ from clan to clan, the largest ones can be found in the hot valley of the Tugela river. Here they measure one metre in diameter and serve as a practical protection against the sun. Before the wedding the bride's friends straighten her hair which has grown long and apply herbs to protect the hair against vermin before the hat is sown onto it. Now the hat can no longer be taken off and will slowly rot on her head over the next few months. There-after her hair is washed and the procedure is repeated.

The sown-in hat could be compared with a chastity belt. The wife could not possibly pretend to be an unmarried woman during the often long absences of her husband by simply not wearing her hat.

Today, women with a more modern outlook refuse to wear a permanent hat for hygienic reasons.

Skirt:

Another typical characteristic of a married woman is the heavy knee length skirt made of cow hide, or in poorer families a goat skin is used. The erotic part of the Zulu woman's body, the back of her upper thigh, may only be seen by her husband.

In order for the skirt to drape correctly, the leather is cut into long strips which are sown together on the inside. The skirt is repeatedly treated with charcoal and animal fat. As fat, however, begins to smell after some time, powdered Tamboti wood *(Spirostachys africana)* is rubbed in to neutralise the smell.

Pregnant women cover their breasts with a beaded antelope skin.

Breast cover:

Married woman wear a cover made of material or skin over the bosom that frequently carries a message in the form of beadwork. This message is only understood by her husband.

isibamba:

While a woman is pregnant, she wears a belt made of dried grass, embroidered with glass or plastic beadwork, to support the additional weight.

Isibamba means *"to help support"* or *"to hold"*.

20

Drums

   Singing and dancing accompanied by drums is a favourite activity among the Zulu people.

   The drums used today are petrol barrels that have been cut open on both side's and covered with goat skin, this style being copied from the kettle-drums of the invading British troops in the past century. Prior to this, large earthen pots covered with a tensioned hide were used.

   Another instrument, known as a vibration drum, is a hollowed container the size of a water bucket, one opening being covered with a skin. A reed is anchored through the centre of the hide, on which the musician tugs periodically with wet hands, producing vibrations of a dull, droning sound that can be heard over great distances.

Message of love. Above the kraal flies a red-white banner as a sign for an imminent engagement party, being an open invitation from the lovelorn man.

DumaZulu (Cultural Village and Lodge)

Duma Zulu - meaning "Thundering Zulu" is the largest Zulu village of its kind on the continent and the only tourist Zulu village opened by King Goodwill Zwelithini - placing the royal Zulu stamp of approval on the objectives and authenticity of DumaZulu.

It is home to sixty four people, including a sangoma *(see page 43)*, spear, shield and pot makers, bead threaders, basket weavers and a team of energetic dancers who do spectacular Zulu dance routines to the sound of beating drums and hauntingly beautiful voices.

A knowledgeable Zulu guide accompanies each visiting group on a tour around the Village. The guide gives detailed explanations and will also answer questions and provide insights into the heritage and culture of the Zulu nation.

The accommodation section of the DumaZulu complex is known as DumaZulu Lodge and consists of twenty units sleeping two to four persons each. Layout of the Lodge is in two circular formations in keeping with African living traditions. The exterior of each unit depicts the diversity of our tribal peoples including Zulu, Swazi, Sotho, Xhosa, Venda, Tsonga, Ndebele and Tswana while the modern interior is tastefully decorated in ethnic fabrics and tribal memorabilia.

DumaZulu
P.O.Box 79
Hluhluwe
3960

Tel.: (035) 562 0144
Fax: (035) 562 0205

Cultural Show Times:
daily
08:15 am
11:00 am
03:15 pm

Evening shows with dinner on request

Flags

In many kraals in Zululand one can find flags in varied colours, hoisted on tall poles. In most cases they indicate their Christian denomination or that beer or meat is being sold there. However, white and white-red flags have a different, more ethnic meaning: white is the traditional colour for love, and where such a flag is raised in full view of everyone, an engagement party is imminent. In the bridegroom's kraal, frequently a white-red flag is flown as a symbol for what the young man still has to go through, to secure his sweetheart's love. The red colour symbolises blood, tears and longing.

Love letters 37

Food

The Zulu people make approximately forty dishes, maize being the staple food, which is prepared in different ways. They are passionate meat eaters, but forced to be almost vegetarians by necessity, as meat is very expensive. Cattle are only slaughtered on very special occasions.

Their main dishes consist of cooked maize, roasted maize cobs, *phutu* (cold, crumbly maize porridge), samp and beans, *amazi* (curdled milk), boiled *madumbis* (tubers) and sweet pumpkin. When available, cooked cabbage, sweet potatoes, tomatoes and onions are also favourites.

The Zulu people are probably the only tribe in Africa that use wooden plates and spoons from time immemorial and do not sit around one communal pot from which they help themselves with their hands. Before eating, hands are washed, on completion mouth's are rinsed out. Eating hastily is despised. The usual beverage is water, milk, tea or sorghum beer.

Stamping the maize.

The Grandmother

Contrary to western culture, the older women take over ever more responsibilities with advancing age, particularly the chief's mother. Men rarely reached a high age as they usually fell victim to an enemy sooner or later, sometimes even killed by their male offspring when their first grey hairs became visible, this being a sure sign of pending senility, and in the opinion of the younger ones, making wrong decisions.

The grandmother has great influence and makes the final decision, unless they concern disciplinary or financial matters. In accordance with her status, she lives in the large hut of the ancestors in the kraal. After her death, the hut stays uninhabited and is only used for meetings and rituals.

History of the Zulu people

Around 2.000 years ago the Ngunis lived in *Embo*, a mysterious and long forgotten land somewhere in central east Africa, thousands of kilometres away from their present home country.

The question as to why they left their country has given rise to many speculations. Nobody knows the exact answer. At any rate, for centuries they moved south with their herds of cattle until they discovered the fertile valleys of Zululand 1.500 years later. Here the clans spread over wide areas, they drove away the original inhabitants who were primitive Bushmen *(San)*, and after they had done so the Ngunis quarrelled and fought amongst themselves for the best grazing lands.

Burning Africa.

One of the new arrivals was the Nguni nomad Malandela with his wife Nozinja. They discovered the picturesque Mandawe hill near present day Eshowe and put up their new home on its western slope. Malandela chose this place not so much for its scenic beauty but rather for the unrestricted viewpoint of the Nkwalini valley situated at the bottom of the hill. From his kraal Malandela not only had a good view of his cattle grazing but also of the game in the valley. Cattle and wildlife abundantly supplied the small family with milk, meat, hides and skins. According to the stories passed on, Malandela, however, could not enjoy his newly found home for long and was soon called to the

Dawn awakens over the kraal.

land of his ancestors. After his burial a rift occurred in his small family and his widow Nozinja with her second born son *Zulu* (Heaven) and the loyal servant Mpungose moved away. Quabe, her first-born son, was left behind as he had cast his greedy eyes upon his mother's small cattle herd. Where the White and the Black Umfolozi rivers converge the three founded a new home, and there Zulu grew up to become a man. When the time had come for him to look for a wife, his mother made the traditional *lobola* (price for the bride) available from her herd of cattle. No father will let his daughter go off with a young man before he has received a certain number of cattle as compensation for the loss of her valued labour. The marriage of Zulu and his bride marked the beginning of a new clan, and all their descendants proudly carried the name of their progenitor. Zulu could not know that he had laid the basis for the mightiest nation in Africa and that all kings until present day should originate from his family.

After Zulu came Punga, then Mageba, Ndaba and Jama. Little is known about Zulu and his successors. Life was relatively peaceful and with each generation the clan and their herds of cattle grew. In the latter half of the 18th century, Jama's son, Senzangakhona became the chief of the *abakwa Zulu* (people of Heaven). Senzangakhona was involved in a brief love affair with *Nandi* (the sweet one), the chief's daughter of the neighbouring Elangeni tribe. In 1787 Nandi gave birth to the chief's illegitimate son named Shaka. Because of his illegitimate birth, the boys of Shaka's age group made his life hell. This was probably the reason for him developing aggressiveness, and he soon had the reputation of a fearless warrior. Shaka invented the *iXhwa*, a spear for close combat, with a short heavy handle and a long broad blade, which was to prove an invincible weapon. After his father's death in 1816, the thirty year old Shaka seized power to rule over the Zulu people. The tribe's territory by now extended 15 x 15 kilometres, and approximately 1.500 Zulus were under his command. All men under the

Sentry on the watch tower.

age of forty had to undergo military service, and in the course of the next few years his regiments attacked all the tribes in the neighbourhood. These tribes were either driven away or absorbed into his young nation. Eleven years later, the tyrant controlled an army of 50.000 warriors with an iron fist, within a radius of one thousand kilometres there were no undefeated opponents left.

Tending the fire place.

In October 1827, Nandi, Shaka's beloved mother, died. The first white people that arrived in Zululand witnessed the ensuing tragedy. 7.000 mourners close to the corpse were massacred within a few hours, the population was condemned to the worst deprivations for a year. Shaka seemed to have lost his mind, the revering love of his people turned into loathing. On 22 September 1828, Shaka was ambushed and killed by his half-brothers Dingane and Mhlangana. Dying he predicted: *"What have I done, Dingane? You think you can rule over this land, but I see already the 'swallows' (white people) arrive. You will not rule when I am dead because the white people are already here."*

Dingane assured his throne by removing all his assumed and real opponents. Indeed - the white people were on their way. Ten thousand determined Boers packed their ox-waggons and left the Cape forever, which was occupied by the hated English. In long waggon columns they trekked to the interior of the country to find a new home and self-determination.

Piet Retief, the leader of one such column, had an eye on fertile Natal, the Zulu kingdom. At an audience, the king promised him all the land between the Tugela and Mzimvubu rivers under the condition that the Boers prove their friendly intentions by taking up arms against the cattle thief, Chief Sikonyela. Dingane could have easily ordered the destruction of Sikonyela and his tribe with his own regiments but in a cunning way he wanted to find out how dangerous the Voortrekkers were. Sikonyela was taken prisoner and admitted his wrongdoing. With the captured 700 cattle, 63 horses and 11 rifles, Retief and his hundred strong delegation went to Dingane to have the agreement sealed. The king was impressed, and under the pretext of a great dance of friendship, he had all the Zulu regiments assemble and then gave the unexpected command: *"Bambani aba Thakath!"* ("Kill the wizards!"). The Boers were surprised and defenceless, as they had left their weapons at the entrance to the royal capital as a gesture of their friendly intentions. After the massacre the warriors were deployed and fell upon the thousand odd, unsuspecting families who were busy laying out their new farms after years of deprivation while trekking from the Cape. Only a few who had escaped, gathered in the security of the deep interior of the country and swore revenge. Ten months later, 464 Boers armed with muzzle-loaders, moved into Zululand. On a tongue of land in the Ncome river they formed a laager *(barricade)* with their 64 ox-waggon's where they spent the day in prayer. On the morning of 16 December 1838, 10.000 warriors surrounded the primitive defence formation on all sides, the massacre only ended in the late afternoon. 3.000 warriors died in battle, the water of the river ran red with blood, only four of the Boers were injured. The battle of Blood River ended the military power of the Zulus and opened Natal to free settlement. The jubilant Boers did not give up, king Dingane had not been captured. However, he was not waiting to be seized. He set fire to his capital, of 2.000 huts and fled to the far north.

Thereafter war broke out among the Zulu people. Mpande, Dingane's younger half-brother, together with a substantial part of his nation, joined the Boers and pursued Dingane. Near the Swazi border the decisive battle was fought, and Dingane fled to Swaziland. He hoped to find protection there, but what he found was death. Mpande was accepted by the Boers as the next Zulu king, and for 39 years peace returned to Zululand.

Mpande's eldest son, Cetshwayo, took over after his father's death in 1873 after having murdered six brothers and half brothers. This man was made of the same stuff as his uncle Shaka, and under his brief rule the people were returned to their former glory. The military rise of the Zulus was watched with suspicious eyes by the few white people who had settled on the other side of the big border river. In the meantime, England had led a war against the Voortrekkers and Natal was under the protection of the English Crown. The cries of the anxious settlers to put an end to the Zulu threat once and for all grew louder and louder.

Leather skirt - symbol of marriage.

On 11 December 1878, the British government finally gave the Zulus an intentionally unacceptable ultimatum: to disband their army within thirty days, to give up their independence, to allow missionaries to work in Zululand and to place Cetshwayo under permanent supervision of an English commissioner at his residence...

War seemed to be inevitable, but Cetshwayo tried all means to convince the English of his peaceful intentions. His imploring fell on deaf ears and on 12 January 1879, the invasion of Zululand began. The British units had been equipped shortly beforehand with the new Martini-Henry carbines from which a shot can be fired every three seconds. They had the Gatling, a forerunner of the machine-gun, artillery and primitive rockets. 27.000 oxen, 5.000 mules and 2.500 vehicles were at the disposal of these modern troops, which, placed in a row, formed a column of 140 kilometres in length. The 25.000 so-called savages on the other side fought with primitive spears and some old-fashioned muzzle-loaders, but with great fanaticism. The battles lasted for nine months. The English suffered embarrassing losses and became the mockery of the world. As a sign of goodwill, Cetshwayo forbade his generals to cross the border river until the end. Only once, in the heat of the battle, his strict order was disregarded and the responsible culprit was severely punished without delay. Who knows how the war would have ended had Cetshwayo pursued the beaten troops. However the English always had their peace on the other side of the Tugela river with all the detrimental consequences for the Zulus. Repeatedly, Cetshwayo sent negotiators to end the senseless massacres on both sides, but without success. On 4 July 1879, five thousand English redcoats overran the royal kraal near Ulundi. On 26 August, Cetshwayo was taken prisoner and banished to Cape Town. The war was won with indescribable losses, the Zulu nation was destroyed in the end. The peace agreement guaranteed the Zulus their continued independence, the Royal House lost its political influence and a British representative supervised all political activities of the chiefs. The Zulu kingdom was divided into thirteen independent chieftains, thus resembling in theory the power structure of the late 18th century before Shaka began his invasion campaigns.

Hut building

For building the igloo-type grass huts (*iQukwane*) the Zulus use long thin rods, tall grass, rushes, reeds, cattle-dung and soil from termite mounds. Wooden rods are collected by men and placed vertically next to each other into the ground, thereby forming a circle with a diameter of about three metres. At the top they are joined with rushes to form a dome. A hip height half-circle serves as the entrance. In the centre the otherwise unstable structure is supported by a thick branch. Women complete the rest. They collect and then weave dried grass into thick mats and cover the latticed structure with them in several layers. Split reeds are braided into fingerthick ropes, which are knotted like a wide mesh around the grass roof to hold it tightly together. The older women mix dung with soil from termite

Continued on page 30

African village.

mounds to form a porridge-like consistency. The substance is then spread in a thick layer over the floor of the hut and an oval pan is fashioned beside the support pole to serve as a fireplace. An arched wall of clay is frequently built in front of the low entrance as protection against the wind. During the night a dog is chained up here to keep watch. When the occupants are out, the entrance is closed by means of wickerwork made of branches.

A hut built in this way is a solid home that can withstand severe weather conditions for years. During the hot periods in summer, the interior stays surprisingly cool, and on cold winter nights, a warming fire is rarely needed. The fireplace primarily serves as a source of light and for cooking. There is no chimney, so the smoke escapes through the entrance and the thatch. There is only a foot-depth of fresh air above the floor, and here the occupant sleeps on a reed mat. Vermin and destructive borer have no chance of survival in this smoke filled hut - thereby increasing its life-span considerably.

Layout of a kraal . 34

Intricate detailed thatch work.

Isivivane

Isivivane (Stone heap)

In many places in Africa one can still find small stones heaped up, particularly on tribal borders, at intersections of old foot paths and near the entrance of traditional kraals. Travellers pick up a small stone, spit on it and throw it on the heap. With this gesture, they honour the spirits of the local tribe or the respective village and seek protection for the journey ahead. Only thieves and other riffraff avoid contact with the spirits and bypass an isivivane without observing this custom. However, if they are caught doing so, they will be dealt with accordingly.

Ancestor worship 30
Superstition 55

Inyanga (Traditional healer)

Europeans in their ignorance call the *Inyanga* ("the man of the trees") a witch doctor. Rather - the term, naturopath, herbalist or pharmacist would be a preferable designation for the traditional medicine man of the Zulus.

The constantly growing knowledge in their field is passed on from father to son over generations. From early childhood the latter accompanies his teacher, searching for medicinal herbs and roots to learn about their uses. A rather complex task if one bears in mind that approximately 1.500 species of plants are used. After his mentor's death the apprentice takes over the practice, and he, too, will train his successor.

'Muthi' is the general term for medicine, but is also known as "bark of the tree" or "moonlit nights". The Inyanga usually searches for bark of certain trees on moonlit nights. It has been proven that many trees contain medicinal substances. Over centuries a surprising wealth of knowledge about these substances has been accumulated which, to an increasing extent, is being analysed in western laboratories. Some natural remedies are mixed and cooked with dried snakes, bones or dripping innards to make the medicine more potent. Certain Inyangas not only offer much desired remedies against coughs or stomach upsets but misfortune, unhappiness in love, AIDS and lightning as well. Many people who need help are prepared to shoulder any costs and trouble, and undertake long journeys to healers in distant places - similar to modern civilisations. According to investigations, approximately eighty percent of the black population in South Africa consult their traditional healers in all matters of life.

"Doctor's room" of an Inyanga.
Master and apprentice.

Sangoma
.... 14

Kuleka ikhaya (Permission to enter a kraal)

Surely, you would not enter uninvited into someone's home - similarly one does not simply walk into the kraal of a Zulu family.

Close to the entrance the unmarried sons of the chief live, the eldest being responsible for the main entrance. He sizes up strangers, sends away those who are not welcome, lets others wait for an appropriate length of time, and ushers in family members and those who are welcome. Newcomers will experience an impressive welcoming display, known as "*siyakuleka ikhaya*" ("greeting the home"). The gatekeeper proclaims, in a loud voice, endless praises of the chief. If you could understand Zulu, you would be well informed at the end of the spectacle about success, courage, wealth and the number of wives of the respected head of the family and his ancestors.

Sharing a joke while Chief Byiela wait's for the return of his cattle.

A visitor may feel honoured if the chief personally appears at the entrance to welcome the guest. Guests are offered sorghum beer as a sign of welcome.

After his father's death, the gatekeeper takes over the leading position in the family. Performing his duty at the entrance, he has come to know all people with whom his father entertains a relationship as well as those whom he rejects. Therefore, he can carry on the affairs of his family and safeguard their interests without delay or problems.

Kwabhekithunga (Cultural Village and Lodge)

Kwabhekithunga was not build as a commercial enterprise. It is the tribal home of Mbhangcuza (Thomas) Fakude and his family.

By nature, the Zulus are a polite and sharing people, and Thomas and his family welcome you into their home.

The structure and social order of an Umuzi *(Zulu village)*, traditional dress, regalia, hut building, and the role of women and children are all explained.

To celebrate your visit the Umuzi women will create an elaborate meal of six succulent traditional dishes, served with fresh fruit.

Dave and Wendy Rosenhahn, who have been working with Zulu families in the area for years, personally accompany all tours which are conducted by prior bookings only.

Overnight accommodation is available in traditional Zulu "beehive" huts, fitted with electricity, showers, and toilets en suite for your comfort.

Catering, licensed bar and swimming pool facilities complement the relaxed and informal environment, with hiking trails offering game viewing as well as prolific bird life.

The Fakude family earn their living from making traditional Zulu handcrafts. Basketware, carvings, intricate Zulu beadwork, tanned game skins and traditional weapons are all on display and can be purchased from the handcraft centre at wholesale prices. Visitors are encouraged to browse around the centre and watch these people practising their art.

Perfect balance.

Mystical morning.

33

Layout of a kraal

The Zulus call their home an *"umuzi"*. The word "kraal" is the European term for the rural homestead of a Zulu family.

A traditional kraal is surrounded by two circular stockades and thus serves as a primitive but effective defence structure. The huts are situated between the inner and outer stockade. In the centre the cattle are kept during the night *(a)* and a smaller enclosure is constructed for the calves *(b)*. In areas exposed to danger the fence is made of cut acacia trees, the flat and thorny tops are compacted to form an impenetrable wall thus affording the inhabitants and their precious cattle effective protection against beasts of prey and thieves.

Such an enclosure is usually built on a gently declining slope and, as a rule, has one main entrance *(c)* that is always situated at the lowest point of the kraal. With heavy rainfalls, dung and other dirt is thus washed through the entrance onto the vegetable plot below. Due to the decline no rain water is retained and the bare ground of the kraal dries quickly.

In the case of an attack the weak point of the settlement is the entrance, but as the enemy has to fight uphill the defenders have a strategic advantage.

*Traditional 'kraal'
near Hluhluwe.*

The quarters are used according to a pattern that is the same everywhere in Zululand. The hut on the highest point *(indlunkhulu)* furthest away from the entrance, is occupied by the chief's mother and is the abode of the families ancestors *(d)*. The chief has his own smaller hut behind it, to the right *(e)*. The first wife is allocated accommodation to the left of the grandmother *(f)*, the second wife lives to the right of the chief's hut *(g)*, the third wife to the left *(h)*, the fourth again to the right *(i)*, and so on, always alternating from one side to the other. In the hut to the left of the entrance the unmarried daughters live *(k)*, to the right, the young men *(l)*. The chief's two oldest sons watch the entrance around the clock and check on visitors.

The small huts standing on poles are used for storage and watch towers when the kraal is under threat *(m)*.

| Hut building .... 28 |
| Pits in the cattle kaal .... 40 |

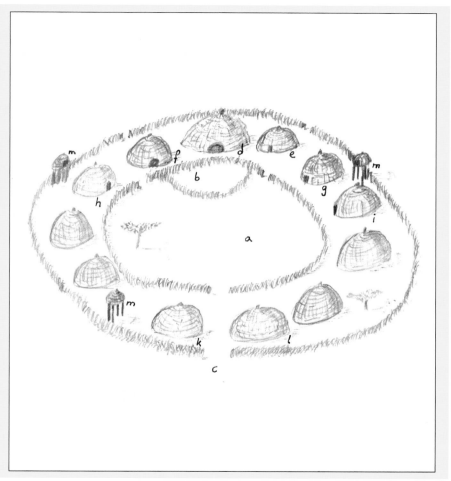

Lightning

Thunderstorms in Zululand are spectacular and frighten the rural population. This is not surprising as every year numerous people and animals are killed by lightning. When a thunderstorm is brewing all shiny objects, water and milk are hidden in the kraal as they "attract" lightning. The head of the family often hurries to the cattle kraal where he burns certain herbs and beats his battle shield with a stick while imploring the spirits of his ancestors to give them protection.

It is a widespread belief that lightning can be aimed at specific targets by witchcraft and sangomas can prevent lightning from striking, by means of potent medicines. Sangomas put an elixir on sharpened sticks made from the sausage tree *(Kigelia africana)* and place them on roofs. A car tire placed on a roof serves the same purpose as a "lightning-conductor". A Zulu on a journey will look for a sausage tree, and carry a branch from that tree with him, for protection.

A person killed by lightning will neither be mourned nor buried with a ceremony as he or she was killed according to the spirits' wishes. Cattle or other animals killed by lightning are not eaten but buried. The wood of trees that have been felled by lightning is neither burned for heating, used for cooking or any other purpose. A hut that has been struck by lightning will stay empty, sometimes a family may even desert the kraal.

Line of ancestors

Ancestors, many generations back, still play an active role in the life of their descendants and are honoured at festivities, as it is believed that no good can be derived from an ancestor who has been forgotten. To be remembered, he might take his revenge by inflicting disease and misfortune. As a preventative, regular offerings are made and songs of praise directed towards the heavens. Through these living customs the Zulus are able to trace back their genealogical tree over many centuries.

Africa's gold - water.

Lobola (Dowry)

For a woman it is an insult to be married without *lobola*.

"*Lobola*" in a laymans term, means - "*Give cattle for a bride*" - which the groom has to pay to his future father-in-law. Strictly speaking, the Zulu man is not buying a wife but compensating her father for the trouble of her upbringing and the loss of her labour. More importantly, he is ensuring the continuance of his blood line with her reproductive ability.

If a wife proves to be infertile or dies before giving birth, then her father is obliged to make a replacement available without demanding more cattle.

Today the bride price is at least the value of eleven cattle, for a young woman of average standing. The more cattle paid, the better the marriage seems to work in the long-term, as the bridegroom frequently has to save over several

Indaba - Meeting.

years for the lobola and therefore chooses his bride carefully.

No wife will dare to oppose her husband as she would be sent home, and her father would have to return most of the cattle.

Polygamy 41

Love letters

Like many other tribes in Africa, Zulus love colourful beads which they work into the most interesting geometrically designed patterns. Particularly young girls like to adorn their graceful bodies with colourful bracelets, headbands, necklaces and embroidered miniskirts. Western jewellery is of little interest to the Zulu people and a girdle of richly embroidered glass beads is preferred to any diamond.

The many different coloured ornaments also fulfil another purpose - they are messages. Young women wearing beadwork in certain colour combinations, renders information of either having reached marriageable age, her engagement, wedding, pregnancy, birth of a child, grief, death and many other sentiments.

Girls in love invent romantic love letters in the form of a colourful string or a small rectangular ornament which is sent to the man of her choice. He will wear this token of her love proudly around his neck, visible to everyone.

The strings are read from one end to the other, the letters from the outer edge to the centre. A white bead represents love and honesty, black stands for mourning, loneliness and disappointment, pink means poverty, green symbolises lovesickness or jealousy, blue represents loyalty, a red bead means tears and desire, yellow signals wealth, and striped beads indicate doubt.

Beadwork 8

Beadwork - silent messages.

Love life

The method of *uku-hlobonga* resembles normal sex, with the difference being that the penis does not penetrate the vagina but rubs against it. This practice is common amongst young men and maidens, to eliminate sexual tension. Parents tolerate this custom as long as the partners come from unrelated clans.

Women who appear too eager, fall under suspicion of wanting to entice the man into marriage, under the pretext of love, or of intending to land the subject with another man's child. If a man becomes too passionate and forces full intercourse, the wrongdoer does not only have to pay a beast to the father, he may even suffer dire consequences by the numerous female friends of the woman he has ravished. In all probability, an unmarried woman who falls pregnant, will be ostracised by her family and friends. The fault, however, always lies with the dishonourable lover.

The higher the social status of a Zulu man, the greater number of woman he marries. Perhaps it would be more correct to say: the more wives a Zulu man takes, the greater the respect will be from his tribe.

However, a dissatisfied wife means trouble and, therefore, the husband either enjoys great potency or is particularly well-versed in the art of love-making. It is the conjugal responsibility of the husband to ensure that all his demanding wives experience

A bride wears leopard skin and a veil.

orgasm without necessarily experiencing one himself. To the Zulu man this is the recipe for successful happy polygamy. At any rate, his prestige as a man, depends on it.

Of course, King Shaka put everyone to shame, as he controlled a completely screened harem of not less than 5.000 concubines, and only one known unwanted pregnancy occurred.

Musical instruments

The Zulu people love music and a fair part of the day is spent singing and dancing. Apart from drums and a primitive bow-shaped string-instrument (*unkluvyana*), no other musical instruments have been developed.

Nguni (Tribe)

The word 'Nguni' is the generic term for all tribes in Africa speaking Zulu or a similar dialect. This includes the Swazis living further north and the Xhosas in the south.

Names

When a child is born a name is given by the parents, which frequently refers to an important event that took place shortly before or after the birth. This explains first names like "Crowning", "Lightning" or "Unemployed".

During the course of life, the child acquires numerous other names, in most cases also a Christian name from the Old Testament.

King Shaka, was given the name of a legendary beetle that somehow finds its way into the abdomen of a woman and causes it to swell. According to history, Shaka's father disputed his paternity and attributed the swollen abdomen to the insect *ishaka*. Thereupon the baby was named *uShaka*.

Playing the 'unkluvyana' for self entertainment.

Military affairs

PheZulu (Cultural Village)

Men's work.

Just 35 km (22 miles) out of Durban you can get an insight into the tribal life of the Zulus at the village of *PheZulu*. *PheZulu* means "High Up" and indeed it is high up at the edge of the *Valley of a Thousand Hills*, with wonderful views into this rural land.

You can expect a fun filled half an hour of theatre about a young warrior who tries to conquer the heart of a maiden. After initial difficulties and with the help of a fortune teller there is a happy ending with lots of singing, drumming and dancing. The guests are also invited into the bee hive like grass huts and a guide explains the traditional artifacts, ancestor worship and beliefs.

Three restaurants with stunning views are close at hand and offer diverse menus from a light snack to an ethnic meal.

The large curio shop is loaded with hand crafts, wood carvings, bead work, ... you name it.

The entrance fee also entitles you to a visit to the nearby Assagay Safari Park, known for its huge crocodiles and snakes.

Pits in the cattle kraal

If a kraal burns down, by accident or intention, the occupants would be faced with the catastrophe of starvation, as their food would have been destroyed. For such emergencies the Zulus still construct cistern-like pits in the cattle kraal in which large quantities of maize are stored. For this purpose, they dig a man-sized hole, with an opening that is just big enough for a child to get through. A young boy plasters the inside wall with clay and piles up the maize cobs in lattice-like layers. The hole is sealed with a flat stone and dung eventually hides the chamber. The contents stay edible for years similar to that of a preserving jar.

Polygamy

The tradition of having more than one wife is common among the Zulu people. A man marries as many women as he can, provided he has the necessary number of cattle to pay the required price to his future father-in-law. A man with only one wife, is one amongst many and does not stand out in the crowd. If he has many beasts but only one wife, his manhood may be questioned. The more wives he has, the greater his reputation and influence in society. His power grows with every addition, and although cattle represent his wealth and are frequently more important to him than his wives, it is often the case that the woman he married first instigates for the "purchase" of another wife. Apart from gaining greater respect from her female neighbours, she also desires further help and entertainment in the household.

The women usually get along very well with each other and ensure equal treatment from their joint husband. Each wife runs her own household, cultivates her own fields, has her own milking cows and cooks only for herself, her children and her husband. The first wife directs the fate of the large family along with the grandmother, and also holds her protective hand over the other wives.

Happy couple.

Uli von Kapff

Pot making

Without the use of a potter's wheel, Zulu women form handy, thin-walled clay pots with roughly carved geometrical designs for a better grip. The smaller pots are used as drinking vessels and to carry water, the larger ones, for cooking and brewing.

The potters collect dry clay, grind it finely with a stone, knead the powder with water, to form a paste and roll it into fingerthick sausages. These are then placed on top of each other to form a spiral, pressed together and smoothed with a little flat stone and water. A blazing grass fire is used as a substitute for a kiln. Different colours are obtained, varying from dark red to black, depending on the use of dry aloe leaves or grass in the fire.

Frequently a dark shoe polish is applied.

Church on the historical Mandawe hill.

Religion

Zulu people spend their lives under watchful eyes of the invisible, yet ever present ancestors. Sacrifices are made to the spirits of the fore-fathers, in exchange for protection and recovery from illness. Before the arrival of missionaries, Zulu people had no temples, no priests nor alters, no idols nor gods and no national cult. They believe in witchcraft and the "evil eye" as well as a higher being by the name of *uNkulunkulu* - "the greatest of all great". They share their world with spirits of the ancestors, numerous mountain and forest spirits and with goblins in rivers and deep caves. There are also many animal spirits and sacred snakes that can bring rain. A female spirit, *inkosazana*, makes the maize grow and in spring-time, young maidens perform rituals in honour of her.

Missionaries from America and Europe have spread Christianity among the Zulu people over the past one hundred years. Zulu traditional beliefs are, nevertheless, deeply rooted, and both, traditional and Christian beliefs, are today combined to form a typical African mixture.

Sacrifices

Practically all Zulu people make offerings to the spirits of their ancestors, in the form of slaughtered animals and luxuries, particularly on occasions such as births, coming of age, weddings, funerals, rain, the sowing of crops and harvesting.

Sangoma - Mouthpiece of the spirits.

Sangoma ("witchdoctor")

The guild of sangomas is frequently referred to by many people as that of wizards or witch-doctors. However, these terms do not reflect the facts. A sangoma has nothing to do with black magic apart from the fact that it is fought by them; he or she is rather a respected spiritual healer, psychologist or priest in the community. Sangomas work with roots, herbs, bark, snake skins, dried animal parts and many other things, whereby most of the ingredients have more of a psychological than a medicinal value. It is rather the spiritual cause of an ailment that is investigated and not only the resulting physical defect.

The chosen one.

Similar to reading tea-leaves, the sangoma reveals the past, looks into the future, finds lost objects and ferrets out thieves by "throwing the bones". A sangoma is the wise person in a clan, and behind the veil of superstition is hidden a sound knowledge of people, that frequently leads to correct conclusions. It was for a good reason, that in former times the training of a sangoma took approximately twenty five years. Today, as a rule, the training period covers a span of five to seven years - in cities, frequently only several months, which may lead to dubious practices that harm the good reputation of the profession. A sangoma does not choose the profession but is rather called to this mission by spirits.

It is the sangoma's life work to keep the community together, to ward off evil and to ferret out unsocial individuals. Beyond this, a sangoma may lead a normal existence, that is, he or she may marry, have children, and if necessary have a second occupation.

Shaka Zulu (King)

Africa's bloody tragedy began on a normal hot day, where Senzangakhona, the chief of the unimportant Zulu tribe, noticed Nandi bathing in the cool waters of the Umlathuze. He did not have to court the pretty daughter of the leader of the related Elangeni tribe for too long, and a love affair of grave consequences developed.

When Nandi's extending belly could no longer be overlooked, her clan sent out a messenger conveying the shameful news to the Zulus. But their suspicious elders replied: *"Impossible! Tell the girl that she is carrying an ishaka in her intestines and not the chief's child!"* (In the Zulus imagination "ishaka" is a beetle-like parasite living in the intestines of some women, that causes the belly to swell gradually. This can be mistaken for pregnancy.).

However, six months later, Nandi gave birth to a healthy baby boy and this time, her powerful father sent a delegation with the threatening demand: *"Here is your beetle! Take it - because it belongs to you!"* Now the elders thought it a wise decision to accept paternity, and Nandi with her infant became the Chief's third wife without any ceremonies. The child was named uShaka. It was the year 1787.

Shaka was an unwanted child, his birth had been the consequence of Senzangakhona's and Nandi's lack of self-control when they had enjoyed *uku-hlobonga* (joys of the way), the Zulu love play.

When Shaka was six years old, he tended his father's cattle and due to negligence a roaming dog killed a new born calf. Senzangakhona was angry with his son. Nandi defended him and as a result of the quarrel she was ordered to leave the kraal immediately with Shaka. Nandi took refuge with the Elangenis, but her illegitimate son had a hard time with the boys of his age. Shaka's greatest problem was his rather small penis, which caused constant taunting by his playmates. By the time he turned thirteen, he passionately hated all and everything to do with the Elangeni tribe. At this age he also did his first heroic deed - a large black mamba killed the best bull of the tribe. Shaka pursued the snake fearlessly, caught it and killed it. For this courageous act the Chief rewarded him with a goat.

Two years later, a severe drought occurred, food was scarce and the tribe could no longer feed everyone. Shaka was sent to the related tribe of the Umthetwa, where for the first time in his life, he was given a friendly reception. Like all the other boys of his age he made himself useful by tending the cattle of the king. One day, a leopard was stalking the herd and the young boys ran away in great excitement, to alert the warriors. Shaka stayed behind on his own and armed only with two spears and a club, he challenged the feared beast of prey.

44

At a distance of fifteen metres, he hurled his first spear, but the leopard was only wounded. No wild animal in Africa is more dangerous than a wounded leopard. When the spitting beast prepared to pounce and kill him, Shaka calmly took his remaining spear into his left hand and the club into his right. Just before the large cat landed on him Shake drove the thin blade deep into its side, simultaneously crushing its skull with a powerful blow of the club. Shaka proudly placed the dead beast at the feet of the Umthetwa monarch. King Dingiswayo recognised the military ability of his fearless charge and the young man entered the ranks of the warriors.

Years later, Shaka did not think much of the traditional combat methods, he had his own ideas. He did not hurl his throwing spear at a great distance, like the other warriors, but he ran towards the enemy, hooked his large shield into that of his opposition, pulled it to one side and plunged his spear into the exposed upper part of the body of the surprised opponent. *"Ngadla!!!"* ("I have eaten"), from then on, a thousandfold, this was to be his cry of victory.

None of the existing spears were suitable for his revolutionary single combat, as the handle was too long and not strong enough. Shaka designed a spear with a heavy short handle and long broad blade naming it *"iXhwa"*. Correctly pronounced, the word reflects the slurping, smacking noise of the blade being pulled out of a body.

Hut under construction.

In 1816, when Shaka was thirty, his father died and the favourite son, Sigujana, was to take over the leadership of the Zulus. With King Dingiswayo's permission, Shaka marched with fifty warriors under his command, to his fathers kraal where he murdered his half-brother and proclaimed himself as the first king of the Zulus. With this action the relatively peaceful times in southern Africa had come to an end. Shaka took terrible revenge on those who had treated him or his mother badly, and he immediately began to build up his own military forces. The Zulu tribe comprised of approximately 1.500 people and their small realm only measured 15 x 15 kilometres. All men up to the age of forty were called up for military service and had to undergo vigorous training. Shaka enforced his own military ideas and equipped the warriors with the new close-combat spears. His vision was a unified kingdom, with him as the sole ruler. All tribes who did not submit to him were wiped out.

The black Napoleon spared the young girls and boys because with them, he could increase his death dealing hoards. "Win or die!" was the motto and those who were accused of cowardice in front of the enemy could be sure of a terrible execution. Shaka proved to be an ingenious tactician and strategist, never repeated in Africa to this day. With cunning he defeated opponents who were considerably stronger in numbers. Twelve years later fifty thousand invincible warriors marched under his command through southern Africa. More than one million men, women and children were slaughtered in his name. The name 'Zulu' was the horror of southern Africa and the mention of Shaka caused panic. He did not hunger for land or the control over nations. His insatiable hunger was for another wealth of Africa - cattle. Shaka's own herd comprised of fifty thousand snow-white beasts, the number of cattle owned by his nation could be counted in hundreds of thousands.

Leopard skin - sign of power.

At this time of turmoil the Europeans arrived. In 1825 a small brig sailing up the coast was shipwrecked on the unpopulated shore of Natal. The surviving members of the crew comprised some big game hunters, adventurers, merchants and a nine year old boy. The landing of the "strange creatures from the sea" was, of course, not kept from the tyrant, and he ordered the *umlungus* to *kwaBulawayo* ("place of killing"), his royal residence. Here the survivors were presented with a spectacular view. Shaka's capital resembled an ordinary oval Zulu kraal, apart from its size, comprising of some one thousand five hundred grass huts and extending eight hundred metres in diameter, this being the largest settlement in southeast Africa at that time. Situated at the highest point, lay the "forbidden" village of the royal family and the concubines. Fifty gigantic huts covering a length of four hundred metres afforded their occupants with a grandiose view of the city. These magnificent grass huts with their polished dark red floors were screened by a 2.40 metre high wooden fence from anyone wanting to peep in.

One of the travellers entered into his journal: *"...Our party were received by King Shaka in a friendly manner, but with that air of haughty indifference which might be expected from the Napoleon of Eastern Africa, before whom everyone was prostrated. A hundred thousand warriors, whose victories had annihilated nations, who had fought in fields saturated with the blood of their slain comrades, knelt at his feet, and to them his words were as the mandate of their deity. Our present excited neither pleasure nor curiosity. He received it with listless indiffer-ence, causing it to be thrown aside, and commenced a desultory conversation, asking questions of King George's dominions, if he had as many cattle and as many warriors as he had, expressing his wish to be on friendly terms with King George, and would give his white people every attention; repeating that if any of them gave them any offence or insult, he would kill them all, men, women and child..."*

During his entire life the warlord proved to be the friend and protector of the whites. The fact that the strangers from the sea, even spared the useless life of a criminal among them, drove Shaka all the more to protect these subjects of the other great king (George). Once he remarked: *"...if it was not for me I fear that there is scarcely an umfokazana (a common man) who would rejoice of having the opportunity to kill all my white people. Oh! They are a bad people; I am obliged to kill*

Sky painting.

a few to gratify the rest; and if I were not to do it, they would think me an old woman, a coward, and kill me themselves. I have been often told by my Indaba (Council) to kill you wild beasts of Umlungus. How happy King George must be, as king of the white men, to me. I see and feel that you are a good and superior people; a strange, a wonderful people. If I understood writing, I would write to King George, and tell him all that I feel, and what I think of the Umlungus (white people)."

In October 1827, the queen died - Shaka's beloved mother Nandi. Within a few hours seven thousand mourners were massacred close to the corpse, and the population had to suffer the worst deprivations for one year. Shaka seemed to have lost his mind, and the revering love of his people turned into disgust.

On 22 September 1828, Shaka's half-brothers Dingane and Mhlangana assassinated the forty year old tyrant from behind with an iXhwa.

History .
.........24

Uli von Kapff

Shakaland (Cultural Village and Hotel)

A unique cultural Zulu village built in 1984 for the production of the epic film - *Shaka Zulu*, the greatest warrior and king of all Zululand.

Steeped in history and offering the visitor a diverse Zulu experience of dancing, spear-making, intricate bead work, fearless stick fighting, Inyangas *(page 31)* mixing potions and powerful Sangomas *(page 43)*. The kraal of Shakaland is the home of a few Zulu families, who take pride in explaining their age old customs and culture.

After a visual introduction of the mighty Zulu nation and gaining permission from the Chief to enter into the kraal, the visitor is taken past the Isivivane *(page 30)*, brewery, family accommodation, - anxious with trepidation to be led into the mystical yet magnetic hut of the spirits, each and every process being demonstrated and explained in full.

Chubby children, warriors and bead bedecked maidens meet you along the way, only to eager to teach you their double hand shake in warm greetings.

A night spent in Shakaland affords you comfortable accommodation in ethnically built huts, with private en-suite. Sounds of the night will gently lull you to sleep, and all too soon you'll be heading back down the dusty road, on to your next destination, taking a small part of Africa with you in your heart.

Shakaland
P.O.Box 103
Eshowe 3815

Tel.: 035 - 4600 912
Fax: 035 - 4600 824

Shields

Shields made of cowhide play an important role in the cultural life of the Zulu nation. They do not only use shields the size of a man, but also smaller shields for ceremonial purposes and even smaller ones for dancing and the traditional stick fights. The colours of shields can be compared to military badges of rank, as one can recognise from them the bearer's fighting strength and thus respect him accordingly. Predominantly white shields are carried by highly respected warriors. The more black, the less experienced the fighter. King Shaka, as the high commander, carried a white shield with only one small black spot, his crack troop carried shields which were approximately eighty percent white. A regiment of recruits was equipped with black shields until the warriors had successfully beaten the enemy in several battles and then received somewhat whiter battle shields.

48

Simunye (Cultural Village and Lodge)

Take a nostalgic trip into the past on horseback or with donkey and cart to one of the most beautiful valleys in Zululand. Mystique and mystery abounds with Zulu surprises on the way to your destination - in what one can only describe as a wonderland of accommodation carved out of solid rock.

A true African welcome awaits you on arrival. Jubilant Zulus in full regalia will astound you with their fierce dancing and outstanding voices that reverberate in the magical hills and dips around Simunye.

Hauntingly eerie, your candle lit evening will be filled with captivating Zulu tales, delightful entertainment and wholesome aromatic food.

Waking up at Simunye is another joyous surprise, preparing to meet the day in true pioneer spirit. After a hearty breakfast you will be whisked away with Vincent, the extremely informative and amusing Zulu guide. Intriguing Zulu showmanship of stick fighting, rituals and customs, Nguni cattle, the local Sangoma and quaint Zulu beehive huts will be the amazing information and sights you can see and hear about.

On your journey up the winding path leading back to your well protected vehicle you will surely wish that you could linger another night in the place that is called Simunye - "We are one".

Simunye Zulu Lodge
P.O.Box 248
Melmoth
3835

Tel.: (03545) 3111
Fax: (03545) 2534

Sleeping

Traditionally, Zulu people sleep on thin reed mats on the floor. A small wooden bench serves as a headrest, today woollen blankets are used instead of skins. If one can afford it, a bed or at least a foam mattress is purchased.

Traditional wooden head rest.

49

Social structure

The Zulu people had developed a well-devised social structure, long before missionaries arrived. They adopted their etiquette, which is based on respect, from the powerful royal family of the nation. Clear rules were defined, regarding duties and manners for the entire royal household, starting with the insignificant water carrier up to the divine monarch. They had precise dictates regarding the behaviour of women towards men, of subordinates to their superiors and of the younger to the elder.

Creating a pattern.

Line of respect in the family

Children learn to show great respect towards their parents and elders from an early age - if necessary with a good hiding as a learning aid. It is the sole duty of mothers to bring up their children, and little ones quickly learn to enter the world of men, only when they have been told to do so. Any instructions given are usually received on one's knees, respectfully and silently, then carried out speedily. In rural areas a young boy will never step in front of his father or address an elder before he has been spoken to first. The young boy also does not show any kind of familiarity, nor does his father. Even men and women keep their distance from each other, living in their own distinct worlds. The role of woman is that of the subordinate one. She lays out the cooked meal before her husband and withdraws to the outside to await the call of her master. Not forgetting the wellbeing of his family, a substantial part of the meal is left in the pots for his wife and children, who finish the remainder in their own company.

Children and their names

A boy is given a few names in the course of his life. After birth, the baby is given his first pet name by his mother, a little later the official name is given by the father. At the age of about seven, the boy is introduced into the group of herdboys and his mates give him a new name. He obtains a further name when he is about fifteen, and on entering the *amabhutho* (local regiment) he was, again given a name.

For girls it is not much different, and almost all add to this variety of names a Christian name as well.

Ready for battle with "shield and stick".

Duties of boys

From the age of six, boys are given chores. It is their duty to look after their fathers' herds. After sunrise they leave the kraal with the cattle and return late morning. After having milked the cows they have breakfast and then go back to the pastures until sunset. On icy winter days the smaller boys are allowed to stay behind in the kraal, the older ones carry out their duties like men. In this way, all young boys spend approximately ten years outdoors, growing up to be strong and healthy men.

Uli von Kapff

Young men and their weapons

Boys learn the art of bloody stick fighting in their early childhood.

In the beginning young cadets hit each other with strong branches, according to strict rules. A stick and small shield to ward off blows is only permitted with increasing age. Until then, thrashings have to be taken with a smile.

Handling a throwing club is part of the training programme. These short clubs with a ball-like top end, are hurled at birds, hares and small antelope; of course, they are also used as hitting weapons.

Boys learn to use the throwing spear by firstly using sharpened sticks. The boys invite each other to go on a rat hunt, the most successful one among them earning the greatest respect. On an occasion of great festivity, ten-year-olds receive their first real throwing spear from their respective fathers, which is small and rough.

At the age of about twelve life became serious. The boys accompanied their older brothers, carrying their loads to the regular military camps. In this way, they were introduced to the disciplined life of the warriors. In the camps, the boys listened to captivating stories of their country, the legends of former kings and unforgotten heroes. Back in their own camps they sang the war songs with high voices and imitated the fiery

Serious training with padded sticks.

dances. They swore to become the heroes of the next generation and were immediately prepared to sacrifice themselves for the ideals of their proud kingdom.

That is how the next generation of courageous and loyal Zulu men were brought up and gave the nation the reputation of the finest race on the African continent.

Target practice.

Showing off.

Growing up of girls

Women are inferior in status and value to the male but that does not necessarily mean that they are treated badly. They are cared for in accordance with their status and are content with their lot.

From the age of five a daughter is gradually introduced to the household chores until approximately six years later when she becomes a real help to her mother. Initially she is given a small gourd and accompanies her teacher to the water source. There the mother first fills her much larger container while the daughter watches and then is allowed to fill hers under the patient supervision of her mother.

Next, the mother braids two head supports (*inkatha*), made of grass, to enable them to carry the load comfortably on their head. The child, not having yet attained the fantastic sense of balance, arrives back well showered and with little water left in her gourd. After a few lessons, she learns the trick and is able to carry the varying loads, even when running without using her hands. This way of carrying loads gives women a healthy and strong back.

Further lessons take place in the field. The child carries a small gourd filled with seeds which her mother hoes into the soil. In time, the daughter learns the correct technique of sowing and hoeing and on her eleventh birthday is given her own light hoe. At this age she knows what firewood to collect, can make a good fire for cooking, prepare some dishes and mind younger brothers and sisters.

A tender moment.

Firing and colouring a beer pot.

Duties and chores of men and women

There are clearly divided household chores and duties between men and women. As in most cultures, Zulu women, too, have been given the less attractive lot.

The man defends his family and his land, takes part in meetings to hear new laws and directives. He receives and entertains guests, puts up enclosures and the basic structure of the hut, carves milking pails, spoons, plates, clubs and spears and if need arises, fetches the traditional doctor. He is in complete control of the possessions and everything belongs to him - his wife owns nothing. The older sons have the privilege to get involved in decision making processes regarding general family affairs. His wife is only occasionally consulted. All business transactions are undertaken by the husband and agreements have no validity without his consent. Everything involving the cattle is exclusively his domain and younger women may not even enter the cattle kraal according to the custom. The Zulu wife looks after the children day and night, cultivates

53

and harvests the fields, collects the firewood, cooks, embroiders, sows and mends, brews the beer for everyday consumption, makes pots, carries the water to the kraal and serves her husband - the list is endless. Men rarely work hard. There is no free time for women and yet they all are happy and content with their lot.

Fetching water - a daily burden.

Power structure - from the kraal to the Royal House

If a family has developed into a large clan it is distributed over several kraals.

In the same way in which each person has a fixed place in the pecking order of a kraal, so the chief of each kraal has a more or less influential position within the structure of the large family. The head of the tribe (*umnumzana*) acts as arbitrator of the clan and usually was a member of the "Lower House". Several of these umnumzanas were placed with their respective districts under an *induna* who decided as a "judge" in more serious cases and had a seat in the "Royal Parliament". Above all indunas in the country, presided the "Zulu Supreme Court of Justice" with its appointed chiefs and ministers. This royal cabinet was the highest authority to which a Zulu person in traditional matters could appeal. Above this is the Royal House, which is taboo.

Utshwala, fermenting sorghum beer.

Sorghum beer

Utshwala is the national drink of the Zulu people. Should you visit a kraal and are not offered any sorghum beer, leave quickly! If you are offered a small pot, drink it quickly and say your goodbyes as you are not welcome. However, if you are presented with a big pot of beer, drink as much as you can and relax because everything is fine.

Sorghum beer consists of maize, sorghum and water. The women are the master brewers and the woman, who produces the best beer, enjoys a higher rank in the family structure.

It is not true that Zulu people spit into the beer to aid the fermentation process.

Stick fighting

Intrigued with the fighting action.

Teenagers and men traditionally settle their personal differences in public with a duel, using fighting sticks *(umTshisa)*. Each opponent holds two sticks of varying lengths, the longer one in the left hand to ward off blows, with a small padded shield to protect the knuckles and in his right hand a carved club with a sharp circular edge at the top, that can crack a skull. The adversaries aim blows at the head and the knees. These bloody and sometimes even fatal stick fights usually take place at big gatherings, such as weddings, in accordance to strict rules similar to boxing matches. Constant eye contact has to be maintained, one is not allowed to strike at the ankles, stabbing is also forbidden and the temper has to be kept under control. An adult acting as referee supervises the duel and declares it to be over as soon as blood flows, which often happens within the first few seconds. The winner tends the wound of the loser and from then on there is no bad blood between the two. Should the outcome be fatal for one of them nobody is charged by the state as long as the fight was fair and took place in accordance with the rules.

Boys are introduced to the art of stick fighting in their early childhood. Initially they train with soft branches and should contact be made, no word of complaint is allowed. Later they use thin harmless sticks. They are presented with the real fighting sticks at the age of about fifteen. In Zululand one often sees men carrying these traditional weapons.

Weapons 56

Superstition

The Zulu people are extremely superstitious. Ghosts, demons, ghouls and witches inhabit every corner of their world. The sangomas have to satisfy an insatiable demand for *muthi* (medicine) for and against misfortune, lightning, courtship, children, success (in the lottery), when job-hunting etc. The list is endless.

All South African football clubs, including the National Team, employ in addition to a masseur and trainer, a sangoma, who is taken very seriously. For example, while chanting incantations the sangoma buries a magnet behind the opponent's goal post in order to attract the balls and he attaches a padlock to their own goal post for additional defence. During half-time he changes them around.

Sangoma 43

Tokoloshe (Demon)

Demons are very real in the life of the Zulu people. It is believed, that wizards *(umthakathi)* use zombies - living corpses - as their slaves in order to spread disease, rape women and kill. The wizard creates a feared tokoloshe by gauging out the eyes of a corpse, cutting out the tongue and driving a red-hot iron through the skull deep into the innards. This treatment causes the body to shrink to that of a child's size. After this, the wizard only has to blow magic medicine into the oral cavity and the tokoloshe is "brought to life" and becomes an eternal slave for his master's evil deeds.

At night, all doors are secured for protection and women place their beds on bricks so that the pygmy-sized tokoloshe is unable to climb onto the bed. A knock on the door by night is answered with silence, as belief goes that whoever answers, is sentenced to insanity, and by opening the door, death is certain.

Weapons

Traditional weapons of the Zulu people comprise of different types of clubs and spears:

Isagila: This is a carved club with a ball, the size of a fist, at one end, measuring roughly 90 cm in length and serves as a projectile. The hunter throws it at large birds and small antelope from about 30 metres away, knocking the prey unconscious, until he can reach it for the 'coup de grace'. This weapon is also used to crush an opponent's skull.

isiPhapha: This is a long throwing spear used when hunting.

iXhwa: A spear with a long, broad blade and short heavy shaft, used as a weapon in close combat.

Deadly weapons.

Swallowtail axe.

umTshisa: A traditional fighting stick that is used to settle all disputes, under supervision. The thin end is frequently tapered to a sharp point and hidden under a tuft from a cows tail. The thick end has been cut flat and the circular edge is sharp enough to split a skull. A second, longer and thinner stick is used to ward off blows together with a small shield for protection of the knuckles.

Battle-axe: This weapon was used not so much for fighting, but rather to identify an induna *(general)*. Indunas only fought each other, ordinary warriors would never have challenged an induna.

Swallowtail axe: It was reserved for commanders of royal descent and only served to direct the regiments in the battle.

Sandals made of car tyre.

Wood carving

Traditionally men carve wooden headrests, milk pails, mortars, wooden plates and spoons.

Masks and figures were only added due to tourism.

Witchcraft

The Zulu people believe that all diseases, misfortunes and deaths are brought about by witchcraft. They do not accept something like fate. A sangoma has to ferret out the evildoer, which in former times led to thousands and thousands of suspects being put to death. Those accused did not doubt that the accusation was justified, as evil takes possession of the body without the knowledge or fault of the person and it has to be driven out by an agonizing death for the good of the clan. Often the family of the guilty person was also put on the pyre, and their belongings became the ever increasing possessions of the chief - who was rubbing his hands in glee. The normal Zulu person who owned more than others due to his business acumen, or whose harvests were better, came dangerously close to being on the black list. A bad omen, such as a hyena near the kraal or something similar, usually confirmed the suspicion, and the next victim for a forthcoming witch hunt had been found. Thus one avoided wealth for a good reason as poverty guaranteed survival for a longer period of time.

Xhosa (Tribe)

The second largest tribe in South Africa, the Xhosas (*ama-Xhosa = the people of the woman*) are neighbours to the Zulus (*ama-Zulu = people of Heaven*). Their tribal land is situated on the southern border of KwaZulu Natal in the province of the Eastern Cape.

Ploughing

Zulu people

The Zulu people have a rich and expressive language with imaginative descriptions and proverbs. They adopted some 'click' sounds from the nomad Bushmen *(San)*, but kept their language purer than those of the more southern tribes. They exchanged news by means of strings of beads of different colours. The written language was introduced by missionaries.

Their body build is rather sturdy than tall, the skin colour rather amber than black, and they are known to be courageous and determined people. A Zulu makes a

Lush Zululand.

good friend or a persistent enemy. They are extremely hospitable, conservative, superstitious, patient with children and incredibly loyal towards their chiefs. Their world is a spiritual arena with wizards, spirits and demons.

The Zulus are excellent singers, untiring dancers and strong drummers.

Zulu etiquette

Greeting

Among the Zulu people the person with the higher standing greets first. A socially inferior person remains silent until he or she is addressed, in order that important thoughts are not disrupted.

Sawubona means "I see you". The answer is: *Yebo, sawubona*, "Yes, I see you, too."

Eye contact

Out of respect, women have eye contact with their male partners in conversation for a few brief moments and then shyly avert their eyes. Long eye contact is considered to be provocative. This respectful attitude is adopted in front of fathers and may even extend to older brothers.

Shaking hands

The traditional handshake consists of three clasps. Initially one shakes hands in the western style, then folds the fingers around the others thumb and finally reverts back to the initial handshake. Depending on the cordiality, this handshake is repeated several times. The left palm of the hand is held under the right lower arm during this procedure.

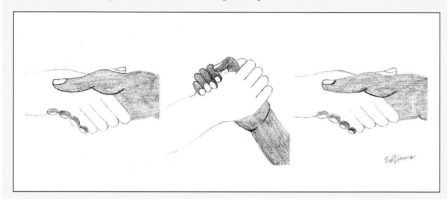

Order in which food is served

First the men are served in order of their standing, then the women and last the children, boys being given preference to girls.

Walking

Women walk a respectful distance behind their husbands.

Men pass on the left of each other. This manner shows each other their strong side - the hand with which they hold their weapon.

Drinking beer

The liberal consumption of sorghum beer plays an important role in the social life of the Zulu people. Beer that has been offered should not be rejected as this means rejecting hospitality. The drinking vessel is held in the right hand, the saucer in the left. As a matter of principle, one drinks either sitting or in a squatting position. Men take off their head cover. Burping *(only men!)*, smacking one's belly or tapping a foot expresses a compliment to the brew-mistress.

Seating order

Nobody sits where he would like to but rather where he belongs. The criteria for seating is sex, age and status.

As a matter of principle, men sit on the right of the entrance to the hut, the eldest or most important person being seated furthest from the entrance. On the left, women and children sit in the same order.

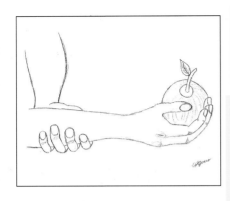

Give and take

Only the right hand is used to give or take. The left palm of the hand is held under the right lower arm during this procedure to show that nothing is hidden.

How does one sit?

It is considered unseemly to sit on the bare floor. One always sits on something like a grass mat, shield or hide.

Men squat with their legs pulled up at an angle, women either pull their feet to the side, close to the hip or they sit with their legs extended in a parallel position.

Zulu family tree

The first large influx of black people in Zululand belonged to the ethnic group of the Nguni who gradually moved over a period of one thousand five hundred years, finally arriving in the late 16th century. Among them was Malandela and his wife Nozinja. They had two sons, Quabe and Zulu (*Heaven*). Quabe was the first born and therefore became the chief's successor. Zulu, together with members of his family moved on and became the progenitor of the Zulu clan. After Zulu came Punga, then Mageba, Ndaba and Jama until Senzangakhona became the leader of the small Zulu tribe in the late 18th century.

Senzangakhona fell in love with Nandi *(the sweet one)*, daughter of the neighbouring Elangeni king who bore him an illegitimate son named Shaka. With him the peaceful and leisurely life in Zululand came to an end. Shaka, the Napoleon of Africa, founded the Zulu nation with its dynasty that exists to this day.

King	Reign
Shaka	1816 - 1828
Dingane	1828 - 1840
Mpande	1840 - 1872
Cetshwayo	1873 - 1883
Dinizulu	1884 - 1913
Soloman	1913 - 1933
Cyprian	1948 - 1968
Goodwill	1971 -

Bibliography

Destruction of the Zulu Kingdom by Jeff Guy (University of Natal Press)

40 years among the Zulus by Josiah Tyler (Struik)

Illustrated Guide to Southern Africa by T.V. Bulpin (Reader's Digest)

Long ago by R.C. Samuelson (Griggs)

Shaka Zulu by E.A. Ritter (Penguin)

Southern Africa: Land of Beauty and Splendour by T.V. Bulpin (Reader's Digest)

The diary of Henry Francis Fynn edited by J. Stuart and D. Mck. Malcolm (Shuter and Shooter)

The Natal Papers of 'John Ross' by Charles R. MacLean (Killie Campbell Africana Library; University of Natal Press)

The Road to Isandlwana by Philip Gon (Jonathan Ball Publishers)

The Social System of the Zulus by Eileen Kriege (Longmans)

The Washing of the Spears by Donald Morris (Simon & Schuster)

The Zulu Kings by Brian Roberts (Hamish Hamilton)

Through the Zulu country by Bertram Mitford (Griggs)

Photographic credits

Leo Kroone, Valley Management cc, © D+J Heaton, page 54 left.

Rob Deane, Gooderson Leisure Corporation, page 6, 8, 9, 34, 50, 61.

All other photography by *Uli von Kapff*

Location

DumaZulu page 6, 8, 9, 16 (b-l), 34, 50. *Kwabhekithunga* page 45. *PheZulu* page 38 (l) 54 (l). *Shakaland* page 4, 5, 10, 13, 14, 15, 16 (t+r), 17, 18, 19, 20, 21, 23, 25, 26, 27, 29, 30, 31, 32, 33 (r), 37, 41, 43, 46, 49, 51, 52, 53, 54 (r), 56, 57. *Simunye* page 12, 38 (r), 39, 40, 55, 58 (l). *Zululand* page 5 (l), 24, 33 (b), 36, 42, 47, 58 (r), 61.

Drawings

Ilala Weavers page 6

Warren Green page 7, 41, 59, 60

Uli von Kapff page 35

Positone DTP Design and Repro page 65

Index

Glossary

amabutho - local regiment
amashoba - tufts of cows' tail
amazi - curdled milk
Elangeni - former tribe
Embo - mystical land in Africa
Eshowe - former capital of Zululand
ibeshu - apron covering the buttocks
ilala - sleep
Indaba - council
indlunkhulu - the big hut
induna - general
inkheswa - small hollowed gourd
inkosi - chief
inyanga - herbalist
iqukwane - igloo-type grass hut
iquthu - basket for grain
isagila - throwing club
Isandlwana - second stomach of a cow
isichumo - drinking vessel
isinene - front apron
isiphapa - hunting spear
isivivane - cairn of small stones
ixhwa - spear for close combat
kraal - village
kwaBulawayo - 'place of killing',
        Shaka's first royal capital

laager - barricade of waggons
lobola - dowry
madumbi - edible tuber
muthi - traditional medicine
Nguni - Zulu speaking tribes
phutu - crumbly maize porridge
sangoma - spiritual healer
siyakuleka ikhaya - greeting the home
tokoloshe - zombie
Tugela - 'something that startles'
ukhamba - clay pot to drink beer
uku-hlobonga - petting
Ulundi - 'the high place'
umlungu - white person
umnumzana - head of a tribe
umthakathi - wizard
Umthetwa - former tribe
umtshisa - fighting sticks
umuzi - home of a family
unkluvyana - musical instrument
unkulunkulu - 'the greatest of the great', God
uShaka - legendary beetle
uthswala - sorghum beer
Voortrekker - pioneer
Zulu - heaven